T0021541

**FIND OUT WHAT
YOU CAN BE WHEN
YOU GROW UP!**

The Big Book
OF JOBS

Pavla Hanáčková, Hana Mokrošová,
Helena Haraštová & Elena Pokaleva

Albatros

Contents

HOBBIES

We all have hobbies. Some of us like sports. Some of us read books. Some of us enjoy singing. In short, everyone is interested in something. What one person finds boring can be loads of fun for someone else. Which is great! In many cases, our hobbies influence what we choose to do when we grow up.

HARD WORK

If you really enjoy something, it is worth putting your heart and soul into it. Doing your best to make your wishes come true can be pretty tough, however. Vets, for instance, must know every little thing about animals' bodies. They must study a lot to be ready for the demands of the job. But when they cure an animal patient, they feel on top of the world!

FOLLOWING YOUR DREAMS

Sometimes, grown-ups stop enjoying their work. As we humans are inquisitive and quick to learn, we are forever finding new hobbies. It is not unusual for an office clerk to realize their dream of opening a stall selling delicious ice cream. Indeed, this ice cream may be better than that of a trained ice cream maker who works only for the money.

A HOBBY CAN BROADEN YOUR OPTIONS

A person who likes music may not be a talented singer. This doesn't mean that they should give up on their passion. There are many occupations connected with music, and this person may excel in some of them. They might compose songs for other singers. They might become a live sound engineer, whose work allows the audience to enjoy a concert to the maximum. All occupations contribute to the whole. We all play a role in bringing joy to others.

A DREAM JOB

What would you like to be when you grow up? Everyone gets asked this question. Many children dream of becoming a teacher, an actor, a doctor, a firefighter, a police officer, or an astronaut. Come with us and find out what interesting, even fascinating, jobs you can do if you enjoy the following things...

2. Are you interested in COMPUTERS?

Are you creative? Do you favor a screen and a mouse over a canvas?

Do you understand computing, and can you help others solve their computer problems?

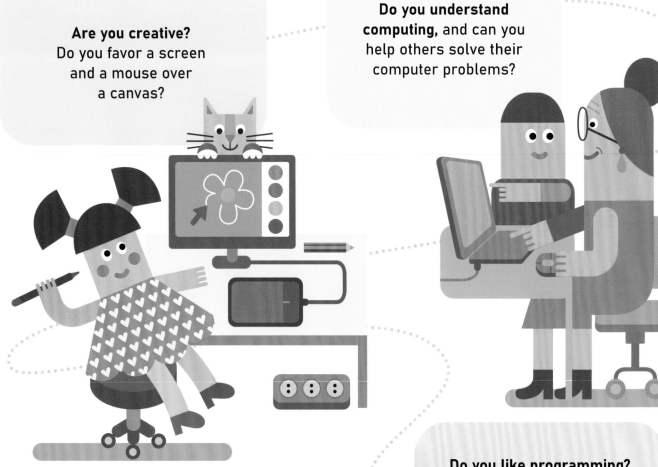

Do you like programming? Are ones and zeroes your friends?

WHAT YOU CAN ACCOMPLISH:

- creating a fun computer game

- editing music for a blockbuster movie

- inspiring others

- modeling landscapes filled with cliffs

- protecting others against attacks from scammers

HTML </>

0010
1001
1100
0010

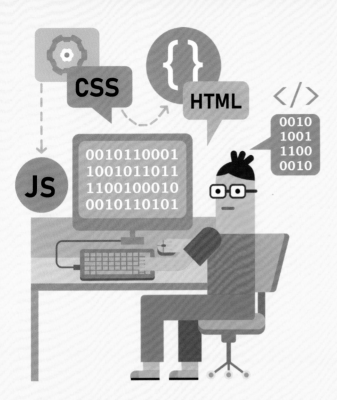

PROGRAMMER

A programmer is responsible for various programs and applications. They create them using the code of a given programming language. Commissioned by clients, they work on projects, which they devise, modify, and test.

INFORMATION SYSTEMS TECHNICIAN

This technician has a perfect understanding of computers and how they work. They work in a team that takes care of the set-up, security, and repair of technology and internet services for companies. People come to them for help whenever there is something wrong with their computer. Sometimes they give advice over the phone; sometimes they visit the customer.

COMPUTER ANIMATOR

A computer animator uses a computer to make images, objects, and texts move so that in the finished film they appear to be moving on their own. Some animators create all figures and objects in advance. Others work with things provided by a director or art director.

WEB DESIGNER

A web designer designs attractive, clear, functional websites for companies and individuals.

CYBER SECURITY SPECIALIST

Like a soldier, they protect us against our enemies, using computers and their knowledge of programming instead of weapons.

GAME DEVELOPER

A game developer designs new computer games.

NETWORK ADMINISTRATOR

They are responsible for the operation and intercommunication of all computers in a company or institution.

DIGITAL TERRAIN MODELER

As commissioned by a client, a terrain modeler creates a digital environment that provides a safe space for training and intervening on unsafe terrain.

APP DEVELOPER

They devise and create new applications for cell phones and computers.

INFLUENCER

They inspire others with the photos, videos, opinions, and comments they publish on social media.

SOUND DESIGNER

They use their ear for music to put together all the music and sound effects for a film or theatrical production.

3. Do you enjoy CARS, AIRPLANES, and OTHER MACHINES?

Do you like playing with toys that move and go?

Do you **stay cool** under pressure?

Do you like to **travel far away?**

WHAT YOU CAN ACCOMPLISH:

• repairing a broken-down car

• designing and building a dancing robot

• playing a part in the victory of your favorite racing team

• building roads and entire towns

• helping others choose the car that suits them best

PILOT

A pilot flies an airplane, helicopter, or other flying machine. Before they reach the cockpit, however, they must pass some very difficult exams. Not only do pilots know all about planes, but they also know about physics, engineering, and navigation too. A pilot must have perfect mental fitness.

SHIP'S CAPTAIN

A ship's captain leads the crew of a ship or submarine and bears full responsibility for its safe navigation. As well as being an expert navigator and weather forecaster, they know a lot about international law—because you can't roam the endless seas without respecting the law.

TRAIN CONDUCTOR

The conductor is basically the captain of the train. They delight in driving their train (whether it's a cargo train or a metro train) to the best of their abilities, alert to whatever might happen. They keep a close eye on the tracks ahead, checking it for any dangers.

MECHANIC

A mechanic repairs and adjusts technical components of machines big and small.

ROBOTICS ENGINEER

They ensure the proper operation and maintenance of robotic stations on factory production lines.

CAR DEALER

A car dealer knows enough about different car models to advise buyers on which one is the exact right one for them.

MAINTENANCE MECHANIC ON A PIT CREW

Traveling the world with the drivers, they look after the repair and maintenance of racing cars.

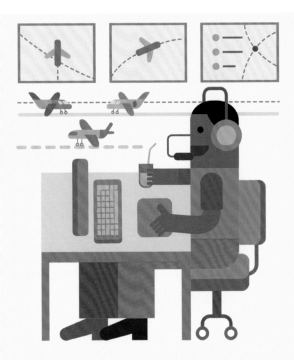

AIR TRAFFIC CONTROLLER

At the airport, they provide pilots with instructions to ensure smooth and safe operations both on the runway and in the air.

VEHICLE DESIGNER

They apply their imagination and eye for beauty to the design of new vehicles.

AIRCRAFT MECHANIC

They work at the airport, making sure all airplanes and helicopters are in good working order.

EXCAVATOR OPERATOR

They operate an excavator on a building site. Along with other construction workers, they make new roads, parks, swimming pools—even whole streets.

4. Are you interested in SPACE?

Would you like to do **what no one before you has done?**

Do you enjoy mathematics and physics? And do people say that you are extraordinarily patient?

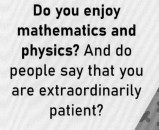

Do you imagine launching your model toys for real?

WHAT YOU CAN ACCOMPLISH:

• discovering life in space

• making a space mission happen

• getting youngsters interested in science

• making a space shuttle comfortable for astronauts

• ensuring that telephones and the internet are working here on Earth

ASTRONAUT

Before joining a spaceflight, an astronaut must endure a difficult training program. They must be brave and levelheaded when handling technical difficulties during their isolated mission. They must know a lot about engineering, and if they're on the International Space Station, they must speak both English and Russian. Among the stars and planets, they represent all of humanity.

ASTRONOMER

An astronomer explores space and cosmic bodies without ever leaving Earth. Using state-of-the-art technology, they see to unimaginable distances, and even into the history of the universe as they watch the evolution of space! What's more, they can predict the future of our planet on the basis of scientific research. Among the stars and planets, they represent all of humanity.

ROCKET SCIENTIST

To design and build space rockets for real, they know all there is to know about physics and mechanics. They are happy to test new approaches and materials to ensure that each state-of-the-art rocket is reliable and safe.

SPACE CHEF

They provide astronauts on space missions with a healthy, balanced diet.

ASTROBIOLOGIST

They search the universe for previously unknown life forms.

SPACESUIT DESIGNER

They make constant improvements to spacesuits, thereby ensuring the comfort and safety of the courageous astronauts.

SPACE POPULARIZER

They work at a planetarium, astronomical observatory, or museum, enthusiastically passing on their deep knowledge of the universe to the institution's visitors.

PLANET SEEKER

Using telescopes with the highest precision, they search for previously undiscovered planets.

ROCKET TECHNOLOGIST

They test and inspect real and model rockets to make sure they are safe to undertake a space mission.

SATELLITE DESIGNER

A satellite designer devises artificial satellites that are placed in Earth's orbit to help people communicate, forecast the weather, navigate, explore space, and spy on enemy states.

SPACE COMMAND CENTER STAFF

A member of this team of experts manages a space mission and communicates live with the space shuttle's crew.

Do you love trying to **solve challenging puzzles?**

Do you often get carried away exploring adventures? And are you happy to get covered in sand or mud as you explore?

WHAT YOU CAN ACCOMPLISH:

- digging up dinosaur bones

- testing new medicines

- working for a healthy future for our planet

- uncovering the mysteries of heredity

- predicting the number of births in the next ten years

Do you want to figure out what animate and inanimate objects are made of?

ARCHEOLOGIST

Adventurers search for historical artifacts, most of which are buried deep in the ground. They conduct research leading to the discovery of old buildings, objects, and human and animal skeletons. As they explore our history, many archeologists travel around the world. They may get to explore the pyramids of Egypt or the tombs of the Aztecs. Items they find are kept in museums and vaults.

CHEMIST

They understand the world as compounds of atoms, molecules, and minute particles that give all things their characteristic properties. In a laboratory, they conduct experiments and observations by which they discover new things about chemical substances. Their knowledge can be applied to many fields, most notably medicine, engineering, and biology, but also bookbinding and the textiles industry.

FORENSICS OFFICER

A member of the criminal investigations department of the police, they document crime scenes and look for clues. With their professional equipment, they take detailed shots that may lead investigators to the perpetrator.

RENEWABLE ENERGIES SPECIALIST

They dedicate their lives to the search for sources of energy that do not burden the environment or harm our planet.

PHARMACOLOGIST

They study the effects of natural drugs and drugs produced in a laboratory.

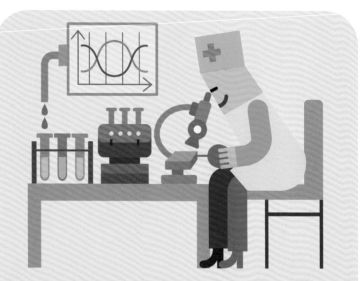

MEDICAL LABORATORY TECHNICIAN

They examine samples of biological materials under a microscope and then analyze them. They also determine the condition of a patient's health in consultation with a doctor.

OCEANOGRAPHER

This daredevil dives to the ocean deep to explore marine life and study the history of the seas.

HISTORIAN

They spend their lives meticulously studying historical sources, thereby revealing as much as possible about human history and learning how history has influenced the present.

PALEONTOLOGIST

These experts study fossils, which tell us about life on Earth millions of years ago.

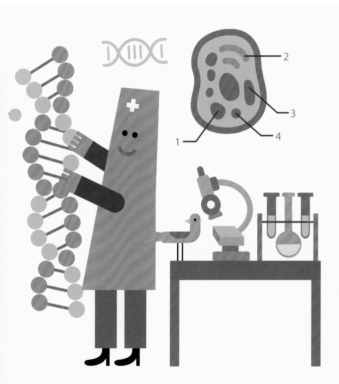

GENETICIST

Through a microscope, they explore human, animal, and plant genes, which carry information about the characteristics and origins of a species.

STATISTICIAN

A statistician analyzes data with mathematical precision, applying logic to derive facts and information.

6. Do you adore BOOKS?

Is your **favorite smell the smell of new books?**

Is your head filled **with thoughts** and original ideas?

Would you like to **pass interesting knowledge** on to other people?

WHAT YOU CAN ACCOMPLISH:

• using books to make complex scientific themes easy for others to understand

• thinking up the next blockbuster movie

• helping young people discover a love of books

• convincing users of your website to adopt from an animal shelter

• writing witty slogans that bring smiles to people's faces

WRITER

A writer has a vivid imagination and a way with words. Many writers produce stories or educational materials. Some prefer to write poems or theater plays. Successful writers travel the world giving readings and discussing their work.

BOOKSELLER

A bookseller transforms their passion for reading into a profession. They must carefully choose which titles to order from publishers for their shop, where the books are then shelved by category. The most popular books tend to be displayed in the window. Some booksellers hold events at which well-known writers meet their readers or new books are discussed.

JOURNALIST

A journalist must be able to write readable, engaging, and convincing articles based on what is going on in the worlds of politics, society, culture, or sport. People turn to such articles to understand things in greater depth. Often, a journalist must acquire information in person, on the spot, by interviewing politicians and experts. This is no job for shy people!

LIBRARIAN

A librarian sorts through and organizes books in a public library. They issue these books to readers who wish to borrow them. The library also holds cultural events.

EDITOR

As creative people with a natural feel for language, editors are in charge of the whole process by which new books get made. They cooperate with the illustrator, the graphic artist, and the author, as well as the production and marketing departments.

SCREENWRITER

A screenwriter comes up with stories, situations, and dialogue for use in films and TV series.

COPYWRITER

A copywriter's head is filled with original ideas. They write the words used in advertisements and promotional materials, which must appeal to as many people as possible.

BLOGGER

Bloggers write about their experiences, opinions, and discoveries on websites or social media, which are available to all for a small fee or even for free.

GREETING CARD WRITER

They come up with imaginative, witty, pleasing words in beautiful script for inclusion in different kinds of decorative greeting cards.

TRANSLATOR

A translator has such a good command of languages that they can translate books and articles from one language to another. Not only is the result identical in content to the original, but it is ideally just as readable and engaging.

PROOFREADER

A proofreader detects and corrects the sneakiest errors of spelling, grammar, and style in a text.

7. Do you enjoy DRAWING and MAKING THINGS?

Do you have an eye for beauty? And do you like to advise your friends on what to wear?

WHAT YOU CAN ACCOMPLISH:

• restoring battered, broken cupboards so that they are as good as new

• making the bride into the loveliest woman under the sun

• becoming the author of the next hit comic-book series, whose heroes save the world

• ensuring that a new book looks and reads well and will attract readers

• turning writing into art

Are you better at expressing yourself in **colors and brushstrokes** than in words?

Do you have lots of **original ideas?**

PAINTER

A painter is a master of art. The works they create include paintings and frescoes. They move freely between artistic techniques, using a variety of tools, depending on what they wish to express. A painter often begins their process by making small sketches to try out ideas; only the best of these will be worked into the final image. People will then admire their work in galleries, and also in the street and in books.

MAKE-UP ARTIST

A make-up artist works in films, theater, or behind the scenes at a concert hall. Their job is to transform performers so that they appear exactly as their role demands. Using special cosmetics, dyes, hairpieces, and other aids, they can change actors' hair color, as well as their apparent age. They can even turn them into fairy-tale creatures and animals!

DESIGNER

A designer must have a vivid imagination. Part of their design work involves creating new forms for a variety of objects. Some are decorative, others are practical. Designers help make new furniture, décor, and fittings on public transport, and they are even active in virtual reality.

RESTORER

A restorer uses a variety of techniques to restore old art objects, paintings, furniture, and even entire buildings.

ILLUSTRATOR

An Illustrator works closely with the author of a book, creating pictures that complement the book's plot.

CALLIGRAPHER

A calligrapher is a master of using beautiful handwriting to create text and inscriptions for books, greeting cards, invitations, and posters. Sometimes they even create new fonts.

BOOK DESIGNER

A book designer is responsible for a book's appearance. It should be attractive and pleasing to the reader, and it should reflect the book's textual content.

TATTOO ARTIST

Using tools with sharp points, tattoo artists draw permanent pictures on people's skin, usually following a design of their own selected to reflect the customer's interests.

COMIC BOOK ARTIST

A comic book artist combines imagination, artistic talent, and a feel for good writing to produce exciting stories in graphic form.

COSMETOLOGIST

They are trained in beauty treatment for the hair, skin, and nails. They make up brides, models, and anyone who wishes to emphasize their best features.

STAGE DESIGNER

A stage designer is in charge of the design and realization of costumes and scenery for TV, film, and theater productions.

8. Do you like to EXPRESS YOUR CREATIVITY?

Do friends provide you with entertainment as you **attempt your own artistic creations?**

Do you let your **imagination** run wild?

Can you tell which **colors and shapes go well together?**

WHAT YOU CAN ACCOMPLISH:

• preserving important moments in history with your camera

• ensuring that the latest book by a respected writer reaches its readership

• making a pirate's treasure chest

• designing the dress that a future queen will wear at her wedding

• drawing up plans for redeveloping a neglected area of the city

HAIRDRESSER

A hairdresser has an eye for beauty, which they put to practical use by cutting and styling hair. They know which colors, shapes, and styles will suit each individual. They can tell who will shine with an eccentric array of hair colors and who looks best with a simple haircut in a single shade. Some hairdressers enter competitions to show off their art.

JEWELER

Using high-precision tools, a jeweler designs and makes soulful objects that add beauty to the wearer—no easy task! A jeweler's workshop can be in operation for generations. Whether they work with metal, wood, stone, or plastic, a jeweler must have an eye for fine detail.

FLOWER ARRANGER

They see flowers as objects of beauty from which works of art can be made. They produce beautiful bouquets for weddings, graduation ceremonies, and other special occasions. Their arrangements will animate and brighten up any surface or space.

PHOTOGRAPHER

They make their living by capturing images and creating professional photographs of people, animals, objects, and events, sometimes traveling great distances to do so.

CABINETMAKER & CARPENTER

These artisans use planes, saws, grinders, and chisels to make furniture, windows, doors, and even staircases.

PUBLISHER

They manage the process by which new books, magazines, and newspapers are put on the market.

CERAMICIST

From sculpting clay, they make pots, figurines, and sometimes small items of jewelry.

ARCHITECT

An architect applies their powerful imagination and technical expertise to designing buildings, interiors, and sometimes even whole streets and parks.

DRESSMAKER & TAILOR

They stitch, adjust, and repair clothing for anyone and any occasion.

FASHION DESIGNER

They design and sometimes make original clothing for fashion shows and everyday wear.

3D GRAPHIC DESIGNER

On a computer monitor, they design and produce various models of objects and places.

9. Is **MUSIC** your best medicine?

Are you unable to imagine your life **without songs or musical instruments?**

Are you patient? Is "diligence" your middle name?

Do you long to stand before an audience?

WHAT YOU CAN ACCOMPLISH:

• making the party swing on the dance floor

• composing a hit that people will sing on their way to work

• helping a beginning guitarist choose the right strings for their instrument

• making the sound of thunder using only two metal plates

• ensuring the smooth running of a concert with thousands of fans

SINGER

A singer has a lovely, trained voice that requires everyday practice. They have the most fun at work during concerts, at which they appear with a band or other accompanying musicians. They may become a star of TV or the theater, and they may release their own album. If they are successful, they will acquire a ton of fans!

PROFESSIONAL MUSICIAN

They play a particular musical instrument so well that they can perform solo, with a band, or as part of an orchestra. Sometimes they write their own songs. When they travel the world to perform for their fans, they have a team of great people around to transport the instruments and manage the sound and lighting at their performances.

CONDUCTOR

The conductor is the indispensable leader of an orchestra. They stand with their back to the audience facing the musicians, who follow the conductor's instructions as they play. A conductor's other responsibilities include staging and adapting compositions, plus working with directors and choreographers.

COMPOSER

They apply their imagination and emotions to the rules of harmony to create new songs and melodies.

DJ

A DJ (which stands for "disc jockey") plays music at weddings, clubs, and parties, where they play the music through speakers, choosing the playlist according to the audience's mood.

RADIO DJ

On their radio programs, they play parts of songs, conduct interviews with famous singers and other musicians, and say interesting things about music.

MUSIC MANAGER

A music manager has a great understanding of the music industry and the singers and bands they work for. They make sure that concerts sell out and recording sessions go well.

MUSICAL INSTRUMENT SHOP OWNER

Their understanding of both business and musical instruments allows them to help customers with their choices.

MUSIC TEACHER

While they provide children and adults with a musical education, they try to pass on their love of music to their pupils.

SOUND EFFECTS TECHNICIAN

They create sound effects for film and theater. For instance, by knocking coconut shells together, they make us think of the clatter of horses' hooves.

SOUND TECHNICIAN

Using technology, they make sure that a concert's audience hears every instrument on the stage well, and also that the musicians clearly hear each other's playing.

10. Do you enjoy DANCING and SHOWING OFF?

Is it fun for you to train regularly?

Does movement make you happy?

WHAT YOU CAN ACCOMPLISH:

• jumping through fiery hoops on a motorbike in front of delighted spectators

• making the grumpiest person laugh

• giving children a fun afternoon

• conducting an interview with your idol

• conjuring a rabbit from a hat

Can you hold people's attention and make them feel happy?

DANCER

A dancer makes a living simply by dancing! They perform in theaters and clubs and on outdoor stages, sometimes for cameras. Some dance solo, some dance in pairs, others dance in a large troupe. As for the types of dance they perform, the possibilities are endless. Every dancer must take care not to get injured and to stay in excellent physical shape.

ATHLETE

An athlete dedicates their life to a certain sport. In individual sports, the athlete has no one to rely on but themselves. In team sports, a player has teammates to help them. Sports are not only about performing well; cooperation, consideration, honesty, and perseverance are important too. The best athletes make it all the way to the Olympic Games!

STAGE ACTOR

A good stage actor can play a big variety of roles, draw the audience into the story, and use their gifts to make people laugh, cry, and think about things. Future actors complete a demanding course of study, in which they learn to speak well, to present themselves on stage, and to understand what makes their characters tick. If they are very good, they might become very popular.

HOST

Their charisma and communication skills are so impressive that they make hosting various public events and TV programs look like child's play.

MUSICAL ACTOR

As well as being able to act, a musical actor can sing and dance. They demonstrate their talents in theaters and films.

STUNT PERFORMER

A stunt performer appears in TV shows and movies filled with breathtaking, high-risk acrobatic stunts.

FAMILY ENTERTAINER

They work in large hotels and at public events for families, leading the children's entertainment program.

MAGICIAN

A magician can convince an audience that they are making true magic, when in fact they are skillfully performing a well-trained trick.

COMIC

A comic provides entertainment on TV shows and in theaters through humor and charisma.

MIME ARTIST

Mime artists are completely silent actors who express themselves entirely through movement and gesture.

YOUTUBER

A YouTuber uploads videos to the internet showing their life and giving their opinions on various matters. If the videos attract enough fans, they can make a living doing this.

11. Are you interested in ANIMALS?

Are you happy to look after others, even if it is inconvenient for you?

Do you adore all **living creatures?**

Do you have patience and can you wait for your reward?

WHAT YOU CAN ACCOMPLISH:

• diving deep to swim among octopuses and jellyfish to explore how they live

• training the perfect guide dog for a blind person

• finding someone's much-loved, missing parrot

• feeding young monkeys, tigers, and crocodiles

• nursing a wounded eagle back to health so that it may fly again

VETERINARIAN

A vet is very fond of animals and helps them when they have health issues. They treat sick and injured animals, irrespective of whether these are small domestic pets or large animals on farms and in zoos. Most vets have their own clinic, where they perform precautionary examinations and provide vaccinations and all other care an animal may need. Sometimes a vet is required to perform an operation, which can be either straightforward or difficult.

BREEDER

A breeder devotes all their time to animals. In addition to providing for their basic needs, the breeder gives them love, affection, and other necessary care. If the animals thrive, the business expands. Some breeders specialize in farm animals that regularly provide eggs and milk. Others do this work purely for the love of nature.

WILDLIFE PHOTOGRAPHER

This is a job for true professionals! If their photos are to look natural, a wildlife photographer, as well as being able to handle a camera, must understand the animals they are photographing. To ensure that the animals do not flee from the shot, wildlife photographers must be quick and agile too. Many of them travel the world to do their work.

WILDLIFE REHABILITATOR

They work on an animal's recovery from illness or injury to ensure that it returns to its natural environment as soon as possible.

ANIMAL SHELTER MANAGER

They offer a helping hand to all homeless animals, oversee the running of the shelter, and find new, happy homes for their charges.

PET DETECTIVE

A pet detective searches for pets that have strayed from home. Because animals sometimes get stolen, a pet detective may work with the police.

PET GROOMER

A pet groomer is an expert with fur-trimmers and claw-clippers. They work in pet salons, making dogs, cats, and other pets look their very best.

ZOOKEEPER

A zookeeper looks after the zoo's inhabitants—feeding them, cleaning out their cages, and checking that they are healthy and happy.

PET SHOP SALES ASSISTANT

They sell whatever your pets need. Many pet shops also have animals you can buy or cuddle with.

ANIMAL TRAINER FOR PEOPLE WITH DISABILITIES

This person trains animals to gladly assist people who need their help with everyday activities.

MARINE BIOLOGIST

They work mostly in the ocean, having dived deep to study the lives of marine creatures.

12. Do you live for NATURE?

Is the future of our planet important to you, and are you keen for others to share this priority?

Are you fascinated by the world of plants, minerals, and countryside, which keeps changing all the time?

Are you interested in how the world works?

WHAT YOU CAN ACCOMPLISH:

• plowing through the jungle with a group of like-minded enthusiasts

• growing corn that produces more, thereby feeding more people

• detecting toxic substances dumped into lakes

• uncovering the history of Planet Earth in solitude among the rocks

• preparing a museum exhibition at which visitors are welcomed by the skeleton of a giant T. rex

BOTANIST

A botanist devotes their life to plants, which they study and document in detail. Some of their research is done in a laboratory, some in the field. Such fieldwork may take them to high mountains, primeval African forests, even vast steppes. A botanist's work is very important for human life: plants can be used to make new medicines.

METEOROLOGIST

A meteorologist delights in the weather! It is their job to study Earth's atmosphere and all phenomena that occur within it. They perform their work from weather stations, where they forecast the weather of the next few days, weeks, and months. The findings of meteorologists are presented in reports and on various weather apps.

CONSERVATIONIST

A conservationist fights against all the harm that humans inflict on nature. To determine how we should treat our planet better, they study a lot and cooperate with various experts. They initiate activities such as the mass collection of waste in forests and the cleaning of watercourses. Many of them lead special interest groups about nature conservation, for children and adults alike.

NATURE GUIDE

They organize group walks and trips during which participants learn about natural phenomena, plants, interesting animals, and how to treat the natural world.

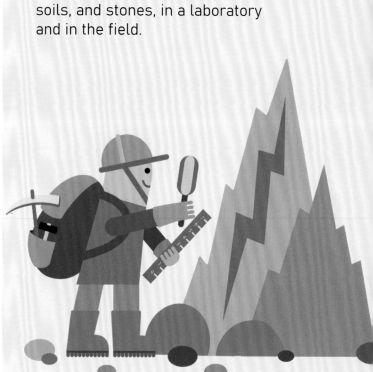

GEOLOGIST

A geologist studies various rocks, soils, and stones, in a laboratory and in the field.

FORESTER

A forester cares for trees, sources of water, and woodland paths to ensure that the forest is healthy and strong.

HYDROLOGIST

A hydrologist is a scientist with a professional interest in water, its composition, and how much of it is in the landscape.

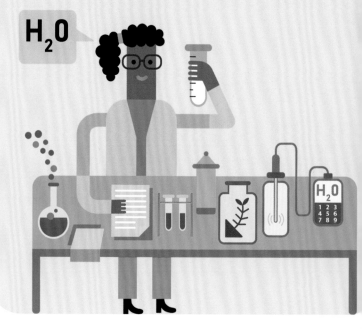

PLANT GENETICIST

They study plants with great expertise before trying to adapt them to meet the requirements of humanity today—by adding vitamins or removing gluten, for example.

PARK RANGER

A park ranger supervises the area of a national park, making sure that its visitors treat nature well—by not picking the flowers or camping illegally, for instance.

NATURAL HISTORY MUSEUM CURATOR

They mount engaging exhibitions on a great variety of topics about nature and natural history. They also guide interested visitors through these exhibitions.

ENVIRONMENTAL EDUCATION COORDINATOR

They work at a scientific institute that holds educational and awareness-raising programs for children and adults—at which, for example, everyone gets to plant a tree.

13. Do you enjoy HELPING OTHERS?

Do you like solving mysteries, and are you unafraid of difficult tasks?

Do you make decisions quickly, and can you **avoid panicking in tough situations?**

Is protecting the vulnerable what you live for?

WHAT YOU CAN ACCOMPLISH:

• defending an innocent person in court

• helping someone get back on their feet after an accident

• shopping for an elderly person and helping them with the cooking

• extinguishing a house fire

• catching a shoplifter

PRIVATE DETECTIVE

This is an occupation for brave souls who don't mind conducting investigations alone. To open a private detective agency, you need a special license. To get one, you need special training and plenty of practical experience. A private detective must be quick-witted and fearless, and they must have good skills of deduction to gather all the information the client needs.

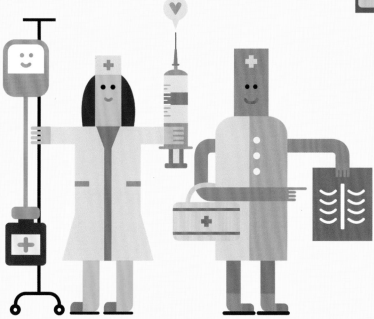

MEDIC

They help sick and injured people back to health. Many medics work on the hospital ward, in the emergency or outpatient department: notably doctors, who diagnose illness, determine treatment, and lead surgery; nurses, who are the doctors' assistants; and paramedics, specially trained physicians who travel out to medical emergencies.

POLICE OFFICER

A police officer should be ready to help and protect others wherever they are needed. The officers in our cities, the traffic police who manage traffic, the criminal investigators who expose and arrest perpetrators of all kinds of crime—all must have keen judgment and treat all people fairly. The police also have a number of special units, employing divers, pyrotechnicians, and pilots, for example.

LAWYER

A lawyer provides help to those with a legal problem, such as the need to draw up a contract or to appear in court.

SECURITY GUARD

This work is for people who are fearless, strong, smart, and fast enough to expose thieves and troublemakers—in stores, galleries, and at public events.

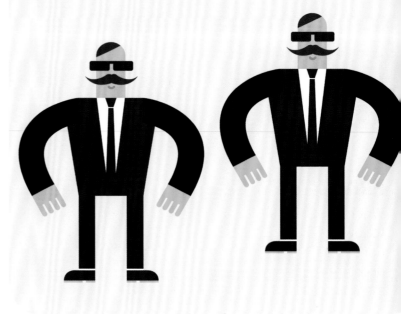

SPECIAL EDUCATION TEACHER

They help children who find it difficult to learn in the traditional way—perhaps because of a physical, mental, or social disability.

PSYCHOLOGIST

Sometimes known as a "doctor of the mind", they talk to people who need to discuss their problems and help them find solutions.

PRIVATE DUTY NURSE

When someone's movement is limited following an accident or illness, private duty nurses help them with their personal hygiene, dressing, and eating, and they also act as a companion.

FIREFIGHTER

A firefighter is always ready at a moment's notice to go to the site of a fire or flood in order to save people, animals, and property.

VOLUNTEER

A volunteer helps out at hospitals, schools, and wherever else a helping hand is needed, asking for nothing in return.

PHYSIOTHERAPIST

A physiotherapist helps athletes and others keep their bodies healthy through special exercises and massages.

Are you happy to teach **someone something new?**

Would you like to see your **efforts lead to visible results?**

Have you always liked **caring for other people?**

WHAT YOU CAN ACCOMPLISH:

• making it possible for people from opposite sides of the world to become friends

• reassuring a frightened passenger on a plane

• arranging a charity ball

• choosing the best candidate for a job

• talking over the telephone to help save lives after a traffic accident

TEACHER

A teacher must have excellent communication skills and be able to explain complex things in a clear, entertaining way. By making learning fun, they hope to motivate their pupils to continue their studies and stay curious. As an educator, they should also listen to what their pupils tell them and help solve any problems. A teacher is a great role model for their pupils.

AU-PAIR

This work is for a responsible person who likes children and is unafraid of adventure. Most au pairs are young people. They go to a foreign country to help with childcare within a family, as a kind of nanny. An au pair helps kids with their schoolwork, thinks of fun things for them to do, and takes them on trips. As they do so, they get better at a foreign language and gain lots of experience.

GALLERIST

A gallerist is surrounded by art—literally! They do their work in a gallery, selecting works of art and arranging them into remarkable exhibitions for visitors to enjoy. To understand the quality of their exhibits, they must know a lot about art. Some gallerists favor the work of modern new talent over the old masters.

INTERPRETER

An interpreter translates communication between two people or between groups, each of whom speaks a different language.

SALES ASSISTANT

They work in a brick-and-mortar shop. They must know a lot about the goods they offer to their customers.

FLIGHT ATTENDANT

They ensure the comfort and safety of passengers on an airplane during a flight. They also serve as a link between the passengers and the pilot.

RESTAURATEUR

They lead a team of cooks, waiters, and other restaurant staff, ensuring that the business works as it should and that customers will be happy to return.

TOUR GUIDE

A tour guide takes tourists to places of interest, such as castles, mansions, national parks, churches, and old parts of towns.

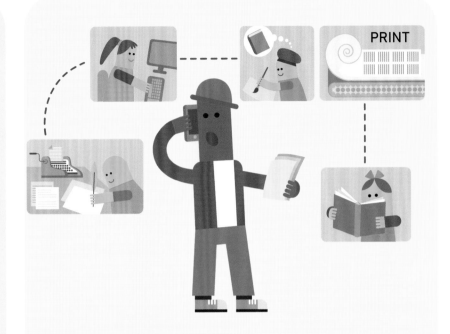

PRODUCTION MANAGER

They manage operations and finances in companies, cultural institutions, and other organizations.

HUMAN RESOURCES OFFICER

They handle work contracts issued by a company or institution, in addition to hiring and training new staff. They also deal with problems that may arise between staff.

HELPLINE OPERATOR

Someone who takes phone calls from people in dire need of medical support and sends out teams of medics must have a background in healthcare, as well as steady nerves.

15. Are you interested in **FOOD** and **COOKING?**

Do you know about different tastes, and do you like trying new recipes?

Do you have a steady hand and lots of patience?

Are you aware that a **good meal can make people feel better?**

WHAT YOU CAN ACCOMPLISH:

• inventing recipes using ingredients no one in your country has ever tasted

• baking the crustiest bread anywhere around

• inventing a strawberry treat that is eaten with a toothpick

• supervising and advising cooks less skilled than yourself

• driving your cuisine to the most entertaining festivals

CONFECTIONER

They make all kinds of sweet things. Sticking strictly to their recipes, they bake and otherwise prepare traditional and original desserts and cakes. As well as being expert bakers, they must be able to make sweet creams, fillings, and tasty icing decorations. Confectioners are good with their hands and very creative.

FARMER

A farmer ensures that a farm prospers and that all who live on it are healthy and happy. They see to the purchasing of animals, agricultural machines, seeds, and animal feed. On a large farm, the farmer hires farmhands to help care for the animals and to plow the fields. We can meet farmers in person at markets, where they sell their products, which include cheese, meat, and flour.

CHEF

A chef prepares a wide range of dishes. An experienced chef is an expert on many cooking processes. Chefs work in restaurants large and small, and some work at top hotels. While some chefs are professionally trained, others rely on their own talents!

FOOD BLOGGER

A food blogger writes about and photographs food to post on social networks. Some of them travel a lot. They wish to inspire their readers to cook.

FOOD STYLIST

A food stylist makes a meal look its best before it is photographed. Such photographs are published in books and magazines and on the internet.

FOOD TRUCK OWNER

A food truck owner carries a small restaurant in their truck, where they prepare good, tasty food for sale at festivals, farmers' markets, or from a regular spot in the city.

BAKER

They are responsible for making and leavening dough and other special processes, resulting in many different baked goods.

MOLECULAR COOK

A molecular cook uses traditional ingredients to make surprising new dishes. Their pots and pans are filled with fragrant, edible chemicals.

HEAD CHEF

A head chef manages a restaurant's kitchen by overseeing a team of chefs. They test the food to make sure it is good before it is taken to the table.

FOOD FORAGER

They travel to different parts of the world in search of new tastes and ingredients, which they bring home and sell to restaurants.

RECIPE AND FLAVOR DEVELOPER

They come up with new (often secret!) recipes for well-known restaurants. In doing so, they look for new flavors to make their dishes as original as possible.

INDEX of the JOBS you can find in this BOOK

The Big Book
OF JOBS

© B4U Publishing for Albatros,
an imprint of Albatros Media Group, 2023
5. května 1746/22, Prague 4, Czech Republic
Author: Pavla Hanáčková, Hana Mokrošová,
Helena Haraštová
Illustrator: © Elena Pokaleva
Translator: Andrew Oakland
Editor: Scott Alexander Jones
www.albatrosbooks.com

All rights reserved.

Reproduction of any content is strictly prohibited
without the written permission of the rights holders.